P9-DKF-885

DATE DUE

DISCARD

EDGE BOOKS

Wild Rides!

Jet Fighter Planes

By A. R. Schaefer

DISCARD

Consultant:
Raymond L. Puffer, PhD
Historian
Edwards Air Force Base History Office
Edwards AFB, California

Capstone press

Mankato, Minnesota

Edge Books are published by Capstone Press
151 Good Counsel Drive, P.O. Box 669, Mankato, Minnesota 56002
www.capstonepress.com

Library of Congress Cataloging-in-Publication Data
Schaefer, A. R. (Adam Richard), 1976–
    Jet fighter planes / by A. R. Schaefer.
    p. cm.—(Edge books, Wild rides!)
    Includes bibliographical references and index.
    ISBN 0-7368-2725-0 (hardcover)
    1. Fighter planes—Juvenile literature. 2. Jet planes—Juvenile literature.
[1. Fighter planes. 2. Jet planes.] I. Title. II. Series.
UG1242.F5S235 2005
623.74'64—dc22   2003027106

Summary: Discusses jet fighter planes, including their history, design, and
    use in military conflicts.

Editorial Credits
Donald Lemke, editor; Kia Adams, series designer; Patrick D. Dentinger,
    book designer; Jo Miller, photo researcher; Eric Kudalis, product
    planning editor

Photo Credits
Corbis, 12; Bettmann, 8, 10, 11; Dean Conger, 13
DVIC, 24–25; SrA Gudrun Cook, 19; SSgt Mike Reinhardt, 18
Getty Images Inc./Sandy Huffaker, 15; U.S. Navy/J02 David Valdez, 4
Index Stock Imagery/Northrop Grumman, 6–7
Lockheed Martin Aeronautics Company, cover, 21
Photo by Ted Carlson/Fotodynamics, 26, 28
U.S. Navy Photo by PH1 Brien Aho, 16; Paul Farley, 22

1 2 3 4 5 6 09 08 07 06 05 04

Table of Contents

Learn about:

CHAPTER **1**

Jet Fighter Planes

A loud roar breaks the night silence. A jet fighter plane speeds across an aircraft carrier. The jet takes off at the end of the carrier. In a matter of seconds, the jet is flying fast toward the coast. The pilot scans the sky and the radar. No enemy planes are in sight. The jet fighter is armed with heat-seeking missiles, just in case.

The pilot continues to watch the sky along the coast. Soon, an enemy plane appears. It is heading for the aircraft carrier. The fighter pilot swoops toward the enemy plane and prepares to fire. Just then, the enemy turns and retreats into the darkness.

The jet fighter plane heads back to the carrier. The pilot makes a perfect landing and turns the plane over to the ground crew for refueling. The jet fighter plane may return to the sky within minutes. It will be ready for more action.

Types of Military Aircraft

Militaries use several types of airplanes. Most air forces have attack planes, bombers, and jet fighter planes. Pilots use attack planes

against an enemy's ground troops. Bomber plane pilots drop bombs on enemy targets. These bombs can destroy airports, bridges, and buildings.

Pilots use jet fighter planes to protect ships and other planes. When fighter planes were first used, their main goal was to destroy enemy aircraft. As air technology gets better, militaries use jet fighter planes for other reasons. Today, many jet fighter planes are also attack planes or bombers.

A U.S. Navy jet fighter lands on an aircraft carrier.

Learn about:

- **The first fighter planes**

- **Jet fighter planes in combat**

- **Variable-geometry wings**

CHAPTER **2**

Early Fighter Planes

In 1903, the Wright brothers flew the first airplane. Soon after, some countries started flying airplanes in combat. Many countries used fighter planes during World War I (1914–1918). The most famous plane of that war was the Sopwith Camel.

The Sopwith Camel

The Sopwith Camel was a single-engine biplane. Biplanes have two sets of wings. The Camel could reach speeds of 115 miles (185 kilometers) per hour. It could fly to an altitude of 19,000 feet (5,800 meters).

Sopwith Camel pilots fought German planes during World War I.

In 1917, British pilots flew the Camel in combat for the first time. It quickly became a deadly weapon. The Camel had two machine guns on its front. Sometimes, a pilot had to fly the plane and shoot the guns at the same time. During World War I, Sopwith Camel pilots shot down almost 1,300 enemy planes.

World War II Fighter Planes

During World War II (1939–1945), some countries started making jet fighter planes. Jet engines powered these new planes. The first jet fighter planes could travel more than 400 miles (640 kilometers) per hour. They could fly to an altitude of 30,000 feet (9,100 meters).

The Germans were the first to use a jet fighter plane in combat. In 1944, they started using the Messerschmitt Me 262. The Me 262 was faster than any other plane at the time. It could fly almost 550 miles (885 kilometers) per hour.

The Me 262 was the first jet fighter plane used in combat.

Toward the end of the war, the Lockheed Corporation built the first jet fighter used by the U.S. military. It was called the P-80. This jet fighter plane could fly more than 600 miles (966 kilometers) per hour. After World War II, the P-80 became known as the Shooting Star.

At the end of World War II, the United States used the P-80 to fly patrols over Europe.

The F-86 was the first jet fighter plane to have V-shaped wings.

New Designs

By 1948, the U.S. military had built the F-86, also known as the Sabre. The United States used the F-86 in the Korean War (1950–1953). The F-86 was the first jet fighter to have swept wings. Swept wings point toward the back of the plane. They form a V shape.

By the 1960s, some jet fighter planes had variable-geometry wings. Pilots of these planes can move the wings from a straight position to a swept position. Straight wings help slow the plane for landings. Swept wings help a plane travel faster during flight.

Other planes have wings that fold in for storage. These planes can fit more easily on aircraft carriers.

Today, many jet fighter planes are also attack planes or bombers. These combination jets can do several tasks. The F/A-18 Hornet is one of the best-known combination jets. F/A stands for fighter/attack. Some countries use the F/A-18 for both fighter and attack missions.

An F/A-18 takes off from the aircraft carrier USS *Nimitz*.

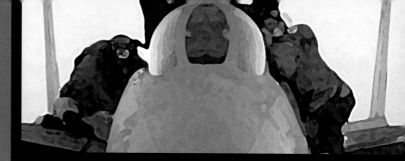

Learn about:

■ **Designer specs**

■ **Refueling**

■ **Joint Strike Fighter**

CHAPTER 3

Designing a Jet Fighter Plane

Jet fighter planes are difficult to design. The planes must be a certain size and weight. Jets must travel very fast and far on a small amount of fuel. Companies also consider the price of building a jet fighter plane. If the planes cost too much, countries can't afford to buy them.

Meeting Specs

Sometimes, a military starts a contest for a new jet fighter plane. They give designers specifications on what the jet should do. These plans are sometimes called specs. Designers use the specs to make models of a new jet fighter. This job may take several years.

Most jet fighter plane specs include weight and size. Weight is important for navy jet fighters. Aircraft carriers have short runways.

The U.S. Air Force uses the KC-135 Stratotanker to refuel jet fighters in the air.

Heavy planes can't build up enough speed to take off on these runways. Size is also important. Small jet fighters can turn and move quickly. They are harder to see in combat than large planes and can more easily avoid enemies.

Most fighter plane specs also include speed and range. Jet fighter planes need to be fast to attack enemy planes. Range is the distance that a plane can go without refueling. Jet fighters must travel long distances on small amounts of fuel. Sometimes, jet fighter planes can refuel in the air. But a plane in combat doesn't have time to refuel.

Tanker planes use a long tube called a boom to refuel jet fighter planes.

Fighter of the Future

In the early 1990s, the United States and the United Kingdom decided to design a new jet fighter. In 1996, they started a contest to design the Joint Strike Fighter (JSF). Several companies competed for the chance to develop the JSF.

In 2001, the Lockheed Martin Aeronautics Company won the contest. Lockheed will build more than 3,000 F-35 JSFs for the United States and the United Kingdom. The jets will replace older F-16s, F-18s, A-10s, and Harriers.

Three models of the F-35 JSF will be built. The JSF for the U.S. Air Force will be an air-to-ground attack and fighter plane. The JSF for the U.S. Navy will have a bigger wing surface for slower speeds. This design will allow the plane to land on aircraft carriers. The U.S. Marine Corps and United Kingdom's Royal Navy will get a different JSF. It will be able to take off and land in small areas.

Some Joint Strike Fighters can take off and land in very small areas.

Learn about:

- **Years of service**

- **Sharper turns**

- **Long-range fliers**

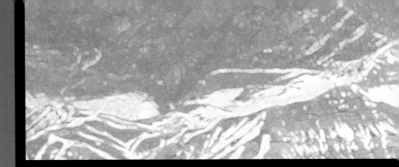

CHAPTER **4**

Famous Jet Fighter Planes

Many countries want to create better jet fighter planes. But current military conflicts are fought with older jet fighters. These planes have proven their usefulness in combat. They have become famous jet fighter planes.

F-14 Tomcat

The F-14 Tomcat is one of the oldest jet fighter planes in service. The F-14 has a top speed of 1,500 miles (2,400 kilometers) per hour. It can fly 10 miles (16 kilometers) above the earth.

In the 1990s, the Northrop Grumman Corporation built the last F-14s. They should stay in service until about 2007. By then, the U.S. Navy will have used the F-14 for almost 40 years.

F-15 Eagle and F-15E Strike Eagle

In 1974, the U.S. Air Force first used the F-15 Eagle. Soon after, they made the F-15E. This combination jet became known as the Strike Eagle. The Strike Eagle is a fighter and an attack plane.

Both models of the F-15 are fast and powerful. They can fly faster than the F-14. The F-15 was the first U.S. fighter plane to have more thrust than weight. This feature allows the F-15 to make sharp turns without losing speed.

F-15s have a top speed of 1,875 miles (3,020 kilometers) per hour.

The Tornado F3 can fly long distances without refueling.

Many countries use the F-15. These countries include South Korea, Japan, Saudi Arabia, and Israel. During Operation Desert Storm (1991), the United States used the F-15 to shoot down Iraqi aircraft. The United States used the F-15E during Operation Iraqi Freedom (2003).

Tornado F3

The Tornado F3 is a European military aircraft. It was designed for the United Kingdom's Royal Air Force. The Tornado has a top speed of 1,480 miles (2,380 kilometers) per hour. It also has a long range. The Tornado can fly far away from base without needing more fuel.

The Royal Air Force used the Tornado F3 during Desert Storm and Iraqi Freedom. They also use the jet fighter to patrol the skies over Europe.

28

F/A-18 Hornet

The F/A-18 Hornet was the United States' first strike-fighter plane. Since 1983, the U.S. Navy has used the Hornet on many important missions. It has become one of the best jet fighter planes in history.

The F/A-18 Hornet showed what it could do during Operation Desert Storm. The fighter plane took off from aircraft carriers. On the way to ground targets, F/A-18 pilots fought enemy planes. After defeating the enemy, they destroyed ground targets.

The F/A-18 Hornet has become popular with militaries around the world. In 2003, it was the only fighter plane used by the Royal Canadian Air Force. Australia, Spain, Switzerland, Finland, Kuwait, and Malaysia also use the Hornet.

Glossary

aircraft carrier (AIR-kraft KA-ree-ur)—a warship with a large flat deck where aircraft take off and land

altitude (AL-ti-tood)—the height of something above the ground

combat (KOM-bat)—fighting between aircraft

conflict (KON-flict)—a war or a period of fighting

jet engine (JET EN-juhn)—an engine that is powered by a stream of gases made by burning a mixture of air inside the engine itself

radar (RAY-dar)—a machine that uses radio waves to locate objects

range (RAYNJ)—the distance a plane can travel on one tank of fuel

specification (spess-uh-fuh-KAY-shun)— detailed information about something that is built or made

thrust (THRUHST)—the forward force produced by the engine of a jet

Read More

Gardner, Adrian. *The F-14 Tomcat.* U.S. Warplanes. New York: Rosen, 2003.

Graham, Ian. *Attack Fighters.* Designed for Success. Chicago: Heinemann, 2002.

Green, Michael, and Gladys Green. *Tactical Fighters: The F-15 Eagles.* War Planes. Mankato, Minn.: Capstone Press, 2003.

Seidman, David. *The F/A-18 Hornet.* U.S. Warplanes. New York: Rosen, 2003.

Internet Sites

FactHound offers a safe, fun way to find Internet sites related to this book. All of the sites on FactHound have been researched by our staff.

Here's how:

1. Visit *www.facthound.com*

2. Type in this special code **0736827250** for age-appropriate sites. Or enter a search word related to this book for a more general search.

3. Click on the **Fetch It** button.

FactHound will fetch the best sites for you!

Index